A Bible Alphabet

Alison Brown

THE BANNER OF TRUTH TRUST

THE BANNER OF TRUTH TRUST
3 Murrayfield Road, Edinburgh EH12 6EL, UK
P.O. Box 621, Carlisle, PA 17013, USA

*

© Alison Brown 2007

*

ISBN-13: 978 0 85151 963 0

*

Typeset in Myriad Pro at
The Banner of Truth Trust,
Edinburgh

Printed in the USA by
Graphics TwoFortyFour Inc.

Introducing little children to well known Bible stories

For Barbara
and others like her
who love to teach little children
about God.

a is
for ark

God said there would be a terrible flood all over the earth because of man's sin. He told Noah how to build a huge ark or boat. All the people and animals who would go inside it would be safe.

b is for basket

A little baby called Moses slept in a bulrush basket. It floated on the river, near the bank. His mother had hidden him there. She didn't want the wicked king to find him.

C is for coat

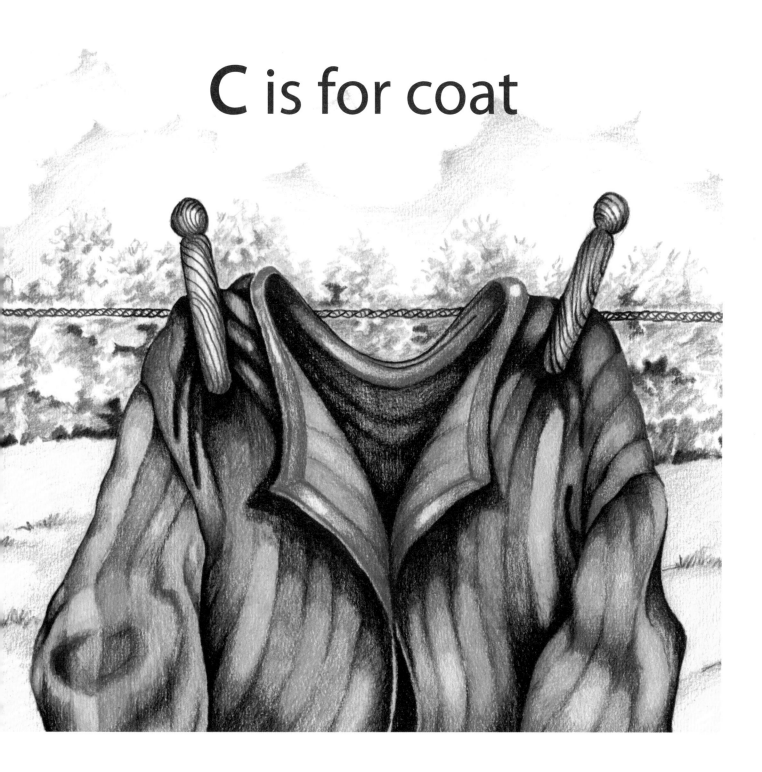

When Joseph was a boy he wore a lovely
coloured coat. No-one else had a coat quite like
it. It was very special. His father gave it to him
because he loved Joseph very much.

d is for donkey

A man called Balaam had a donkey. He got a shock one day when the donkey spoke to him! It was God who made it happen. He wanted to make sure Balaam would listen.

e is
for earth

God made our wonderful earth. He made the skies, the seas, the mountains, the trees and the flowers. He made it just right for people to live in. The first two people were called Adam and Eve.

f is
for fish

Jonah was thrown from a ship into the sea during a terrible storm. God didn't want Jonah to drown so he sent a huge fish to swallow him. Three days later it coughed him safely out on the shore.

g is for giant

Goliath was an angry giant who wanted to fight God's people. David, the shepherd boy, had only a sling and some stones, but God helped him to bring Goliath tumbling to the ground.

h is for house

Mary and Martha were sisters who lived together in the same house. Martha liked to clean the house and cook tasty meals, but Mary loved listening to Jesus.

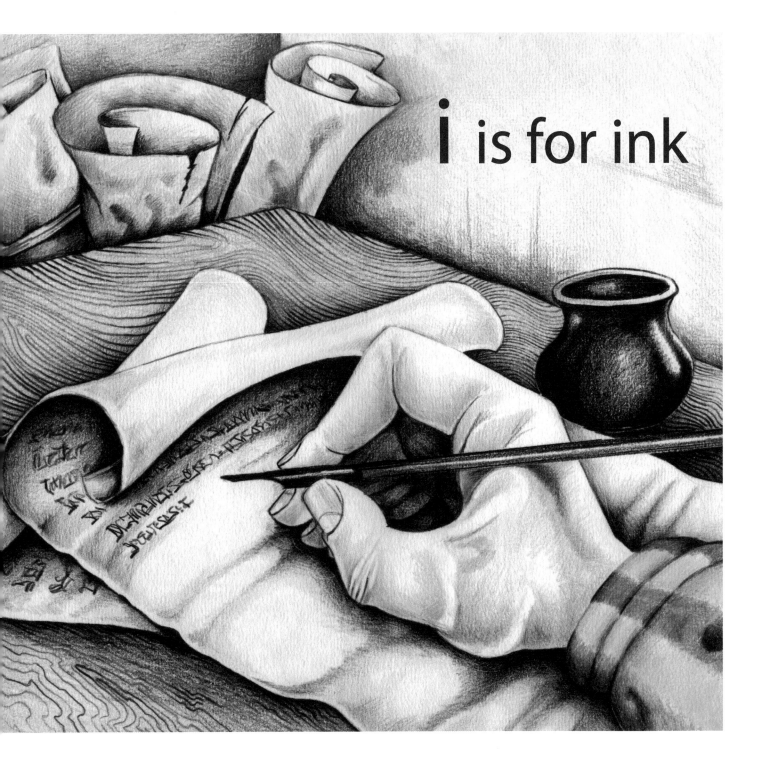

i is for ink

Paul used lots of ink. He wrote many letters to his Christian friends. He taught them wonderful things about God. We can still read some of those letters in the Bible today.

j is for jail

Peter was put in jail even though he hadn't done anything wrong. God sent an angel into the jail to help him. Peter's chains fell off, the door opened, and the angel led him safely outside.

k
is for
king

King Solomon was a very wise king. He asked God to help him make good rules. Some of the wise things King Solomon said are written in the part of the Bible called the Book of Proverbs.

I is for lion

Daniel loved to talk to God, even though it was against the law. That was why he was thrown into a pit with some hungry lions. God took care of faithful Daniel. Not one of those lions touched him!

m is for manger

Mary's baby was born in a stable. He had to sleep on the hay in the manger! His name was Jesus, and he was a very special baby because he was the Son of God.

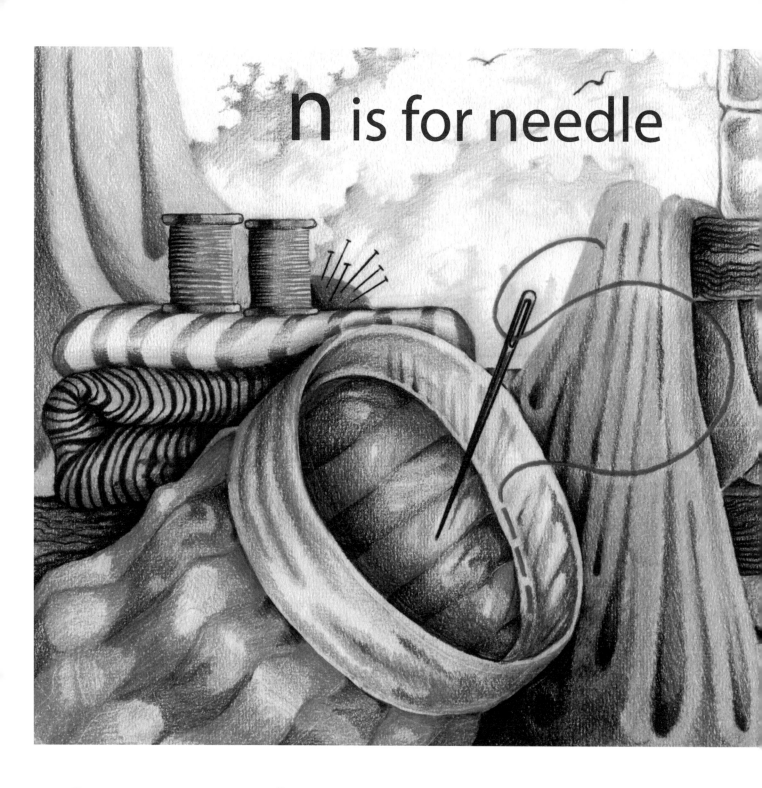

n is for needle

Dorcas enjoyed sewing with her needle. She was good at making clothes. She made lovely coats for all her friends and for the poor people who didn't have any money.

O is for oil

Elisha saw God work a miracle with a little jar of oil. When the oil was poured out of the little jar into lots of big jars it didn't run dry! It just kept on flowing out until all of the big jars were full.

p is for picnic

A little boy gave his picnic to Jesus. Jesus used the five loaves and two fish to feed thousands of hungry people! Everyone had plenty to eat and there was even some food left over.

q is
for
queen

Jezebel was a wicked queen. She took things that didn't belong to her and she tried to turn people away from God. God saw everything she did and he was very angry.

r is for raven

Elijah was hungry, but he didn't have any food. God sent some ravens to feed him. Twice every day they brought bread and meat in their beaks and dropped it down just beside him.

S is for shepherd

Jesus says that he is the Good Shepherd and we are the sheep. He loved the sheep so much that he was willing to die for them. Nobody else loves us as much as Jesus does!

t is
for tent

Abraham lived in a tent while he was travelling. He was going to the new land God had promised to give to his family. Abraham didn't know how to get there, but he knew that God would lead him.

u
is for
unleavened bread

Sometimes God's people ate unleavened bread.
It was flat, hard bread which wasn't very tasty.
They ate it when they were remembering the
difficult times God had helped them through.

V is for vineyard

Naboth owned a lovely vineyard. Big juicy purple grapes grew on the vines. King Ahab lived in a palace next door. Every time he looked into Naboth's vineyard he wished it was his!

W is
for wall

The wall around the city of Jerusalem was broken down. Nehemiah asked all the people who lived there to help him fix it. Everyone worked very hard until there wasn't even one little hole left!

X comes at the end of box

Aaron was the High Priest. He often saw the special golden box that was kept in God's special tent. Inside it there was a copy of God's laws. Aaron knew that God's laws were very important!

y is for yoke

Job was a rich man. He had five hundred yoke of oxen. Job loved God very much. He was able to praise and thank God for everything, even when things went wrong and many of his animals died.

Z is for Zion

Heaven is often called Zion. We read in the Bible that heaven will be a city made of pure gold. There will be no sun or moon needed in heaven because Jesus, the Son of God, will be the light!

You can look in your Bible to find out more:

ark	Genesis chapter 6, verses 13–22
basket	Exodus chapter 2, verses 1–10
coat	Genesis chapter 37, verses 3–4
donkey	Numbers chapter 22, verses 21–35
earth	Genesis chapter 1
fish	Jonah chapters 1 and 2
giant	1 Samuel chapter 17, verses 38–51
house	Luke chapter 10, verses 38–42
ink	Galatians chapter 6, verse 11
jail	Acts chapter 12, verses 1–11
king	1 Kings chapter 3, verses 5–12
lion	Daniel chapter 6, verses 1–23
manger	Luke chapter 2, verses 4–7
needle	Acts chapter 9, verses 36–41
oil	2 Kings chapter 4, verses 1–7
picnic	John chapter 6, verses 5–14
queen	1 Kings chapter 21, verses 1–16
raven	1 Kings chapter 17, verses 1–6
shepherd	John chapter 10, verses 11–15
tent	Genesis chapter 12, verses 1–8
unleavened bread	Exodus chapter 13, verses 7–10
vineyard	1 Kings chapter 21, verses 1–2
wall	Nehemiah chapters 1–6
box	Exodus chapter 37, verses 1–9
yoke	Job chapter 1
Zion/ heaven	Revelation chapter 21, verses 18–27

Also available from the Banner of Truth Trust

A companion volume to Alison Brown's *A Bible Alphabet*, this Activity Book contains 26 large format tear-out sheets which young children will really enjoy colouring-in and completing.

ISBN 978-0-85151-964-7
large format paperback 64pp.

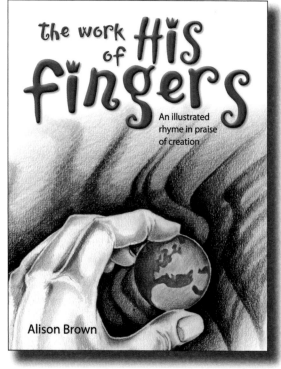

Another beautifully illustrated large format book by Alison Brown. Using a rhyming style which will appeal to the natural sense of fun in all children, the author aims to help the young reader think about the wonders of God's amazing creation.

ISBN 978-0-85151-965-4
large format paperback 32pp